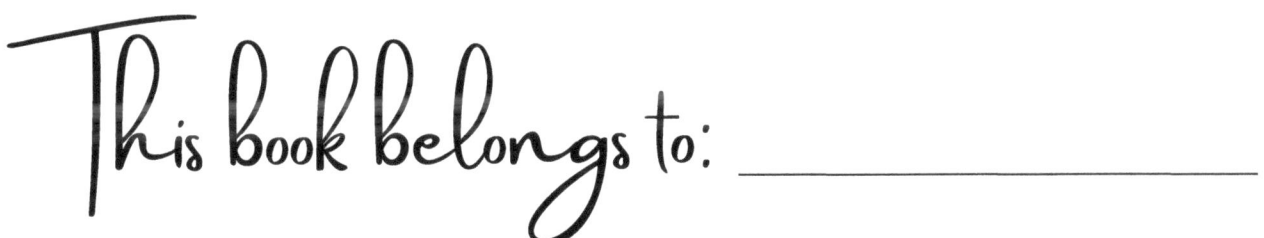

To those who have loved deeply and lost greatly ~ this book is for you.

May you always feel the warmth of their love in the sunshine, hear their laughter in the wind, and find their hugs in the arms of those still here.

Inspired by our sweet daughter:
Caitlyn Alaska Hirschi Wilson

Copyright © Kristine Anne Hirschi, 2025. All rights reserved.
No part of this book may be reproduced or transmitted in any form without permission, in writing, from the author.

ISBN: 979-8-9931638-5-7
Imprint: Independently published

Cover design and artwork by Allie Turek
Families Are Forever artwork by
Hazel Staples @hazel_paints
Printed in the United States of America

Sister, where are you?
I've looked high and low.
Sister, where are you?
Where did you go?

I've been to the playground where we spent our day.

Running and sliding to happily play.

I've looked in the places
that you love to be.
I'm looking for you,
are you looking for me?

We played all the day and had lots of good fun.
Is this hide-and-seek? If it is, you have won.

People say you're in Heaven. But where is that place?

If I knew
how to find
it, I'd hurry.
I'd race.

I'd race to be with you, to be by your side.
Then we'd find a playground… We'd run and we'd slide!

But, I cannot find it.
It's not on a map.

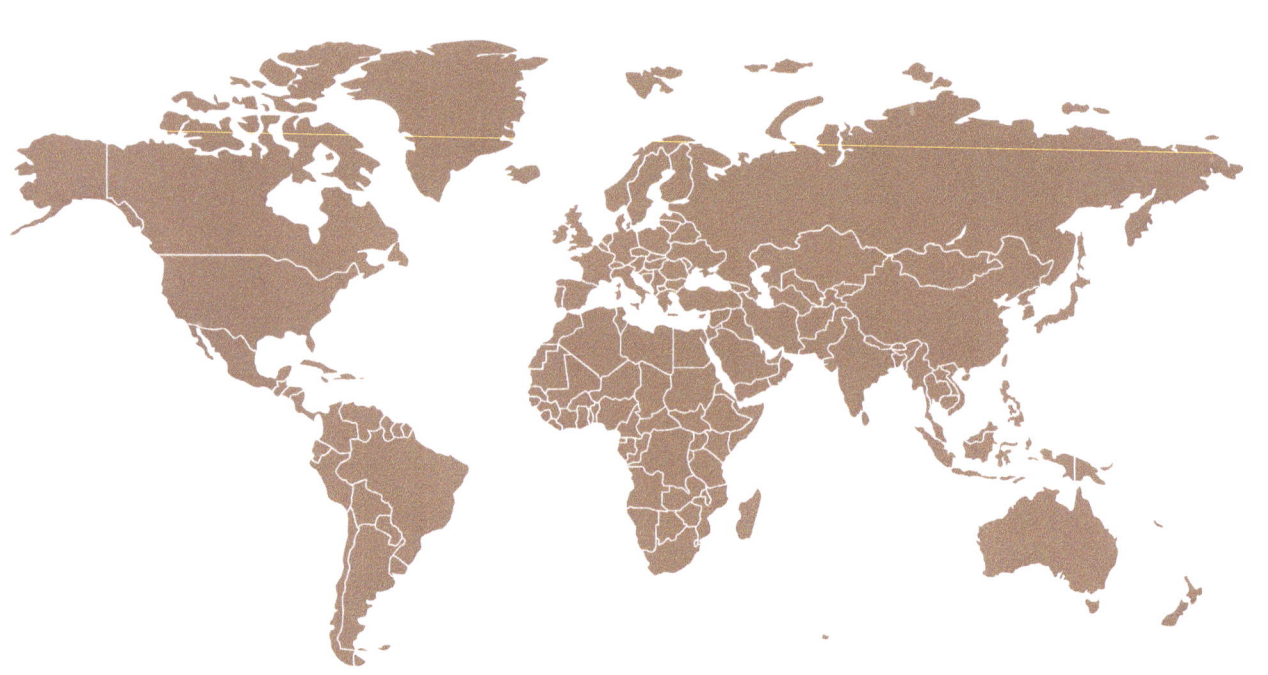

Though I see you in dreams when I'm taking my nap.

*Family, I know Heaven truly is real.
It's a place and a space that for now you must feel.*

It's here and it's there. It is everywhere! A place of pure joy, without any care.

*I know you can't see me,
so trust when I say,
"I promise I'm with you,
every day."*

*With Heaven so close, can you feel that I'm near?
I'm cheering you on. If you listen, you'll hear.*

You'll hear me in windchimes.
You'll feel me in hugs.
All the beauty around you?
That's me giving loves.

A flower that's wild with colors so bright.
When you see them, you'll feel just a bit of my light.

*A butterfly's visit should brighten your day.
When you see it, you'll know that I've come your way.*

*In a sunset with colors,
as bright as can be.
That is me smiling down,
I wish you could see.*

―――――――

*I'm near you.
I know you.
I love you so
much.
Even though
I'm away and
you can't feel
my touch.*

―――――――

*For I am in Heaven,
a place you can't see.
But my spirit is with you for eternity.*

Then one day, I'll see you, we'll run and we'll play.
Then we'll be together, every day!

*I know you can't see me,
but I promise I'm close.*

*So for now
you must
trust that ...*

I love you the most!

love,
sister

Families Are Forever

About the Author:

Kristine Hirschi resides in Hurricane, Utah with her husband, Michael. She is the mother of 8 wonderful children and is "Grammy Shirshi" to 14 grand-children - at the time of this print. Kristine loves writing and recently published a collection of 8 books written in poetry form. She is at the beginning of a promising literary career with many more children's publications ahead.

Sister, Where Are You? is her debut children's book. You can enjoy Kristine's other books in this collection by purchasing:

Mommy, Where Are You?
Daddy, Where Are You?
Grandma, Where Are You?
Grandpa, Where Are You?
Brother, Where Are You?
My Friend, Where Are You? and
My Child, Where Are You?

Each book is written to give children, and adults alike, a sense of peace at the passing of a loved one.

To my dear readers ~

I want to share a portion of my heart with you and tell you how this book (and the entire Where Are You?) collection came to be. You see, in December of 2022 our third daughter, Caitlyn, was due to deliver her second son. Because of severe complications she passed away just 9 days after delivering her perfect baby boy. She left behind her 16-month old son and her 9-day old baby boy along with her husband and countless family and friends who still grieve her loss to this very day. Her husband has married an angel woman who is diligently determined to make sure all of their children know and love Mommy Caitlyn. She is a blessing to us all.

When Caitlyn's oldest son was 3, he came, with his family to visit Papa and Grammy Shirshi. Upon entering the house, he saw a picture of "Mommy Caitlyn". With his big, contagious smile, he turned to me and said, "Grammy! It's Mommy Caitlyn!!"
"Yes, sweetheart, it's a picture of Mommy Cait", I replied, with a lump in my throat and tear filled eyes.
He immediately turned to his daddy and yelled with excitement, "Daddy, Maybe she's here!"
He then began running through my house, room to room, yelling "Mommy, Where Are You!?"

With broken hearts we sobbed as we tried to find the words to tell him that mommy's spirit was here but that he couldn't see her. We struggled to make sense of telling a young child "where" Heaven was, how he could feel her spirit in the beauty around him and even feel her presence.

This moment in time weighed heavily on my heart until in the early hours of a crisp November morning when I was awoken from a deep sleep with the words to a powerful poem pounding my mind. I rose immediately and began writing. When I was finished, the Mommy, Where Are You? poem was born and, from that, this book came to be. In the days that followed, I could not help but feel like these books needed to be shared with others who may be going through a similar situation in their lives.

If you are one of these people, I want to offer my deepest condolences to you, your family and your loved ones. My heart knows yours and I mourn with you in your time of great loss. May Heaven smile down upon you and bring comfort and peace to your soul.
~Kristine Hirschi

www.ingramcontent.com/pod-product-compliance
Lightning Source LLC
Chambersburg PA
CBHW051327110526
44582CB00003B/69